GUYANA
for the **taking** or the **making**?

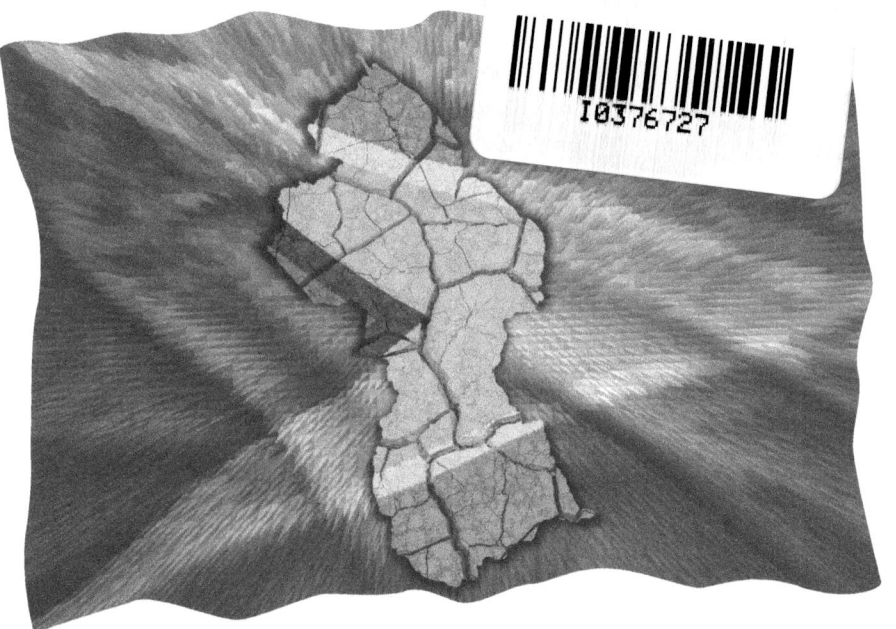

Mahadeo Bissoon

GUYANA—for the taking or the making?
by
Mahadeo Bissoon

published by:
In Our Words Inc./www.inourwords.ca

compiled and edited by:
Cheryl Antao-Xavier

book design:
Shirley Aguinaldo

images:
123RF.com

Library and Archives Canada Cataloguing in Publication

Bissoon, Mahadeo, author
    Guyana : for the taking or the making? / by Mahadeo Bissoon.

ISBN 978-1-926926-72-8 (paperback)

    1. Agricultural industries--Guyana. 2. Environmental policy--Guyana. 3. Guyana--Economic conditions. I. Title.

HD9014.G82B57 2016   338.109881   C2016-906416-6

All Rights Reserved. Copyright © 2016, Mahadeo Bissoon. No part of this book may be reproduced in whole or in part, in any form, or stored on any device including digital media, except with the prior written permission of the author. Exceptions are granted for brief quotations utilized in critical articles or reviews with due credit given to the author.

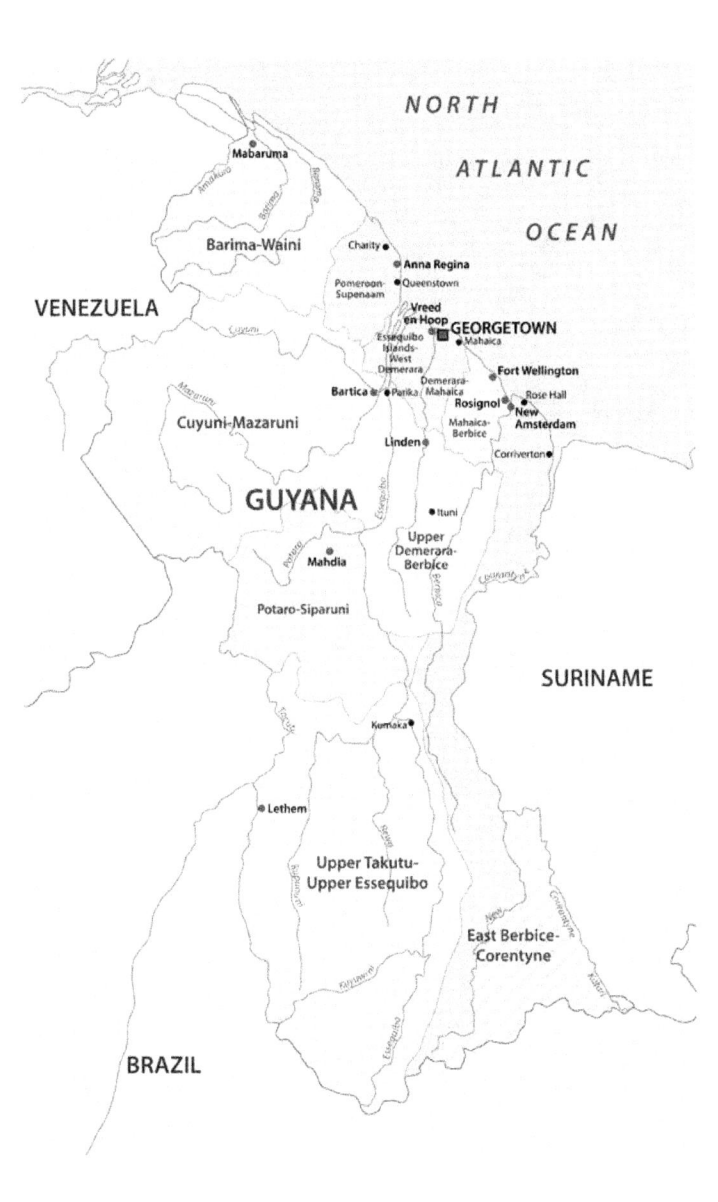

Contents

Introduction 5

Overview 15

Sugar Can Always be King 26

Education – Guyana's Albatross 30

Expansion in Guyana Dairy Activity 34

Coconut and Coconut Processing Guyana 39

Fruit Production 42

The Local Government Elections AND WHAT NEXT? 45

Conclusion 51

Introduction

GUYANA: a country for the taking or the making?

Will Guyana be made or continue to be unmade? There is some chance of realizing the renaissance the new partnership or coalition government in 2015 under President Granger would like. The unmaking followed the 1953 suspension of its constitution and the arrival of British troops and conditions of martial law. This was part of cold war politics which the U.S. engineered in the Americas. Guyana continued to experience a painful traumatic history without let-up even after its independence in 1966.

Much was shredded in the political warfare between Jagan and Burnham who had together formed a political party and then split. The racial divide between the two main population groups – Indo-Guyanese (43%) and Afro-Guyanese (35%) – persists into the present. The racial politics may be lessened through shared power under the current coalition government of five small parties with a slim majority of 51% of the vote. From 1970 the dictatorial politics of Burnham saw the imposition of equally dictatorial economics under his tenure. Ninety percent of the economy was placed under government ownership and control. Bauxite and sugar both declined and the quality and quantity of national life disappeared. Reduced earnings could support neither social services including education and health or infrastructure as earnings went into a downward spiral.

Burnham also loaded the public service, army and police force with Afro-Guyanese to increase his political support and replace Jagan completely. The increased hostility towards Indo-Guyanese and their exclusion from jobs in the civil service forced their emigration. Open racial violence became frequent in Georgetown and elsewhere. This meant a brain drain as many qualified and skilled people left for the U.S, Canada and the U.K. This weakened the entire country in every way.

Jagan's return to power after Burnham's death in 1985 was not long enough to re-balance things. The state had been criminalized as the rule of law had been disregarded. A narco-state emerged with the trans-shipment of cocaine to external markets. Gun violence, murders, human trafficking, and corruption followed with this organized, endemic criminal activity that came out of this deterioration in political life.

Emigration became the option for Indo-Guyanese mainly. It is striking that there are more Guyanese living outside Guyana than in it. It is highest in the world for emigration; close to fifty percent live in the U.S (43%), Canada (31%) and the rest in the U.K. and the Caribbean. The census of 2000 shows 764,000 in Guyana itself. Between 1969-1976 an average of 6,080 left each year and that rose to 14,400 from 1976 to 1981 when Burnham was in power. That has continued and it is estimated between 10,000 and 30,000 in the '80s. Thirty percent of these emigrants took their tertiary education with them, a substantial 'brain drain'. There was of course a decline in the quality of life and guesses can be made about other negative effects. Emigration continues at about 8,000 per year. Conditions have not changed by much.

There was a reversal just after independence in 1966 in the population explosion that was underway due to a rate of increase of 3.5% per year between 1940 and 1960. Guyana went into negative population growth with lower birth rates after this but more important was the effect of emigration. The numbers leaving drained off the increase in population and produced negative population growth. In 1988-89, a negative of –0.5% was reported. This is very unusual for any developing country and the population has grown very slowly by only about 20,000 over the last 50 years.

That deterioration in political and economic life was continued with the arrival of the Jagdeo-Ramotar political leadership. Jagan had won the 'free and fair' elections held with the help of Jimmy Carter and others. After the death of Cheddi and Janet Jagan, the presidency was passed to Bharat Jagdeo and then Donald Ramotar. They floated along on the Indo-Guyanese majority vote and bent the rules of conduct in the affairs of the state. The bauxite operations were partly privatized while subsidies supported sugar activity which continued under state control. Subsidies were extended to rice production and milling which expanded appreciably exceeding the value of bauxite, gold and sugar at one point. Rice is now affected by reduced prices and difficult markets just as sugar and bauxite were before. State assets were plundered with much misbehavior in public office. A great deal of repair work has to be done to return the country to a healthy condition where law is respected and crime checked.

The judicial system and the magistrate courts were politicized.

The most senior of the judges had made a biased decision in favour of Jagdeo's party. It was clear that the state was on a witch hunt under these two leaders. They had singled out anyone who expressed any opposition or disagreement on its action and behaviour. People were being arrested in the middle of the night without explanation or warrant and kept in jail without their day in court. Due process was being denied and a sort of police state had been put in place. The security personnel in the President's office were directing negative attention to journalists who had expressed disagreement over government action. The freedom of the press was being denied.

This government was repeating the autocratic behavior of the Burnham period. The fear of speaking out may have dampened the willingness to debate issues and offer alternatives. This was not as openly brutal as Burnham's regime. Burnham had been responsible or allegedly responsible for the assassination of Dr. Walter Rodney. Rodney had organized a movement that was a threat to Burnham's dictatorial control and racist policy. He led the WPA which became the platform for replacing Burnham. No credibility was given to a costly Commission of Inquiry into Rodney's murder. The report was submitted in early 2016 after much delay. It was pointed out that some key people had not been consulted and their evidence had been left out. The report had failed to implicate Burnham for arranging Rodney's death.

The deterioration of infrastructure, the loss of skilled personnel, the paucity of even basic supplies in schools and hospitals, continued criminal activity, unemployment, rising expectations and the shaky position in so much of economic activity all present a considerable challenge. A comparison may be made to the cleaning of the Aegean stables of Greek legend. Where does one start and which task goes to the top of the list?

How far the idea of a renaissance is shared by President Granger's ministers or not shared may undermine moves to a more honest and self-respecting society in which racial distrust and strife is put aside in the common business of reconstructing an extensively damaged society. There is no shortage of problems and issues that require attention. Some ministers seem conscientious, hardworking and sensitive to problems and needs as they go along. Some do not and offer up statements that make their own self-importance clear – political business as usual.

What is noticeable is the number of Indo-Guyanese who were taking part and expressing their views in a constructive way in the various media lately. This is important too in balancing out the number of Indo-Guyanese involved in questionable practices and continued racism; the majority of misdemeanors coming under scrutiny involved Indo-Guyanese politicians and bureaucrats. The Jagdeo-Ramotar combine headed up the political party based in the Indo-Guyanese majority as indicated above and the security of this majority allowed the abuse of power. This suggested that mixed voices were taking the country to a less racially loaded location. Is it too soon to see a shift away from daily reports of a litany of misdeeds, and news items that read like horror stories that must erode hope and deflect attention from what is possible next? The horror stories are about murders, robbery, arson, suicide, rape and other acts of violence. These are daily occurrences. There was a riot at the main prison in Georgetown in 2016 where the prisoners set fire to mattresses. The prison guards were held off in this overcrowded facility where the meals served were unsatisfactory. There was no water to put the fire out. Calm was restored without violence directed at the prisoners. The exciting business of reconstructing a society and its economy is sidelined as these occurrences show an unstable, insecure social landscape.

When all of the above is set against the economic history and background of the country, the challenges and difficulties of restoring it or in other words to create the renaissance now being articulated and desired seem a very tall order or even a pipe dream. In spite of this, President Granger addresses the country each week on TV. He gives a calm report on the issues receiving attention, a weekly up-date on progress. Attention was also given to the celebration of 50 years of independence and much was being done to make it a memorable event. A positive note is struck as progressive steps are reported all over the country. President Granger himself is doing what he can to get children to school especially where a road network may not be available. He calls this a "boat, bike and bus" campaign to make things easier for children to get to school. Bikes have been found and handed out. Boats have been made available and buses have appeared as they are found. The expression "random acts of kindness" is frequently heard. He is encouraging a breakfast program in the schools while he directs attention for more training for teachers and nurses.

Guyana had experienced a long period of economic decline. It ran up budget deficits and balance of trade payments year after year and again. Over the last 20 years, there has been debt re-scheduling and forgiveness.

One of the last figures shows that $1.8 billion U.S was forgiven. There is still a budget deficit in 2016 and spending on social services and infrastructure appears difficult though unavoidable. Some relief comes from grants from a variety of sources and these seem to keep things going. It is recording a growth in GDP of 3.5% at present and the forecast is favourable for continued growth.

This does not take away or solve the problems of employment and wage increases or poverty; there is much protest from the sugarcane workers in particular. In general, wages have not kept up with the cost of living. There is widespread dissatisfaction among all kinds of workers.

Conventional or Unconventional Strategy

The conventional answer for correcting this deficit situation makes changes to the financial system to correct what comes from such a trade deficit. A fall in commodity prices is cyclical and is a regular, predictable feature of the international market. This affects many developing economies in a severe way. They quite often build their exports and economies on two or three primary commodities like Guyana ignoring the diversification of the economy. The approach may include devaluation of the currency to make imports more expensive and correct this imbalance. Other austerity measures are also put in place. This shrinks the economy and produces reduced employment, frozen wages, and other hardships. While this may be justified as "short term pain for long term gain," the austerity period may last a lot longer before the recession disappears. This causes regular downturns and regular social instability. These ups and downs are undesirable. These commodities use land that some claim should be used to grow more food instead to reduce food imports and make the role of commodities less dominant. Yet the cash earnings from these commodities place even more reliance on trade. Production is increased and makes dependence on trade even more important. This is where diversification of the economy is desirable since it spreads the number of areas that carries the economy and society. Also processing of their products adds more value to the economy and can be met from agro-processing and light manufacturing.

A map for the diversification of the Guyana economy is offered as an alternative to change its current economic landscape or geography. It offers a range of possibilities and with them a wider range of opportunities can be presented to the society. It attempts to offer alternatives to the weaknesses present and looks at what is there in terms of opportunity cost. Opportunity cost means we cannot have it both ways - that is having our cake and eating it. The importance given to trade and especially imports should not be allowed to become an exclusive preoccupation and belief. Imports imply surrendering the chance of producing many of those imports and the jobs, money and technology and capability that that change can clearly bring. At the same time, more foreign exchange must be earned from more exports of the commodities produced. Economic activity becomes narrowed while production diversity is lost. A diagram or model is included and it attempts to capture the linkages between the elements outlined. The linkages both between and within the projects proposed will strengthen the activities and improve the chances of their success if such feed is not implemented. These linkages will be discussed for each proposal.

Burnham had a good idea but he wanted it all done and all at once without understanding any of the complexities. He placed practically all imports on a negative list and pushed the society on a crusade to replace all these imports; this is economic autarky. Soon the shelves in the stores became empty. Prices shot up because of the scarcity created and there was a thriving black market, perhaps the start of the parallel economy mentioned above. It was extreme and it was rather like the shortages and make-do substitutes of Hitler's war time Germany. It was bound to fail because of the many ways in which the society was short on all the skills and resources both human and physical necessary to create such an overnight miracle. Not only was the country short of managerial talent but the "necessity that is the mother of invention" had been taken away from those Guyanese in particular who were placed in a secure berth without the challenge for accountability and personal growth.

It is not intended to repeat those blunders or place blame where blame may be deserved in what is being proposed here. A more practical approach is taken. Things already on the ground are selected to be moved up some notches and developed with the benefit of more experience and research selecting appropriate technology. Some of this was modeled in Guyana at St Sophia and at the government agriculture research unit in Mon Repos. The projects identified are all familiar. They have either declined as in the case of dairying or abandoned as in coconut processing. Nothing impracticable or earth shaking is considered except hydro-kinetic electricity generation. In this case, the innovators who are manufacturing the systems are prepared to include expert installation and training for Guyana to continue running and servicing them. Appropriate technology allows most to adopt them since the machines and tools have been selected for simplicity, durability and lower cost. They do not involve complicated or sophisticated technology but do allow increased production with less raw brute labour. Since the investment levels are modest, economies of scale are easier to meet. Attention must be given to marketing perhaps in a co-operative or group mode to allow some specialization and efficiency. It is also intended that standardization and HACCP requirements are met to allow the products to gain consumer confidence and enhance marketability. Some additional labour may be required in these projects but shared ownership can lead to shared profits and reduced risks. The four selected belong to the agriculture sector:

1. Integrated dairying – mixed farming
2. Coconut processing
3. Fruit production and
4. the related processing of juices, jams, confectionery and so on.

These are discussed in some detail in what follows.

The other area that would bring benefits is in light manufacturing. These projects will be itemized but not developed in any detail since they fall into traditional practice that is well known. They are also straightforward, low cost and require urban locations where industrial parks can be developed. The competition in the production and marketing of durable consumer goods is very strong and countries that have taken this on are hard to dislodge for market share. The products will need quality in design and finish. Consumer satisfaction must be satisfied. Raw materials are easily available and are inexpensive. Here the latest in the machines and technology available may give an edge in production and the market. If any small part of the import market can be captured, that will reduce payments for imports while jobs are created that deliver more than a minimum wage. Sweat shops are not desirable and work places must be improved in the future. More opportunity for improving industrial conditions should come with shared ownership, shared profits and shared decision making. Such changes will place social and economic control in the hands of communities, reduce dependency and reduce conflict. Development must proceed with opportunities distributed on a fair and equal basis without favouring one group over the other.

It is fair to question 'development' that excludes people who are marginalized and not given opportunity to participate in the economic life of a society. They are not empowered as we increasingly chose mega development and mega projects where control and decision making are kept in the 'corridors of power' and behind closed doors. Too many of us are just carried along on this kind of mainstream creation that we become helpless when conditions shrink even for a short period. This kind of helplessness is met with the negative answers of strikes, disruption in production and even violence when dissatisfaction becomes extreme. Guyana is no exception in making violence the one and only answer where conditions become intolerable. It has had a history of that. Alternative answers must be found to counter such a situation. It could be that an answer lies in placing people, the society in the centre of its development, its economy and not the other way around where the tail (economy) seems to wag the dog (the society).

Guyana has too much in both human and physical resources to find itself among the two poorest countries in the western hemisphere with Haiti. In two short generations, the Guyanese who emigrated to the U.S and Canada have made impressive social and economic progress. This is no small accomplishment. The enabling environment in which they found themselves made that possible. It is being suggested that if Guyana itself can be made into an enabling environment, its resident population will be able to exercise its creativity, innovation and risk-taking to produce secure, satisfactory livelihoods. To effect the renaissance currently being raised up as a national goal all the conditions that form this enabling environment must be developed. Many of these conditions must be put in place or strengthened. Most lie inside social and business infrastructure like the ease of doing business without tedious red tape and weak banking services and lending institutions. These are serious drags on getting things done. Some urgency and importance has to be understood and widely shared in the development process.

Guyana's physical resources are diverse and impressive. Its sheer size dwarfs its population, 90% of which is concentrated in the developed coastal region that runs for a distance of 240 miles. This coast lies partly below sea level and gets its protection behind a polder with trenches and drains. Four substantial rivers and several smaller ones drain this region where rice and sugar production cover the fields. The rest of its 83,000 sq. miles is forested or carries savanna vegetation as in the Rupununi. Eight thousand species of plants and a huge array of other flora and fauna add to a complex diversity typical of Amazonian regions. Its timber wealth remains more intact than other regions like it. Its diamond and gold deposits, bauxite and even pure white sand speak to its mineral wealth. Offshore oil and gas reserves are being developed. The intermediate sand hills, the interior mountain region and its Rupununi savanna present some challenges and difficulties for wise use and development. For the last 4 or 5 years, its reliable predictable rainfall has disappeared in the face of uninterrupted drought. There were two wet seasons in an equatorial region with rainfall ranging from 70 inches to over 100 inches. Climate change has fiercely changed that making the future unpredictable in 'the land of many waters.'

The development geographer studies the interaction between the complexities of people and the complexities of place and sees patterns in the distribution of the outcomes. This interaction is now at stake and makes secure livelihoods uncertain. Of people and place, people seem to weigh more heavily in the equation.

In the early 1990's, the IMF was asked to deal with the country's indebtedness and this led to a cut of one third in the public service and a reduction in the number of ministries from 11 to 8. With continuing budget deficits, there will be no increase in employment in the public sector. The private sector shows little sign of expansion and the investment by foreign investors sees much spending on large trucks and machinery with few new jobs. Retail businesses employ many sales people with low wages. A lot of those selling in either Starbroek or Bourda markets in Georgetown are engaged in huckstering or the suitcase trade and tiny stores. These are clearly under-employed people with small sales and low profits. Self-employment offers a solution to this pressure for jobs. Even micro-enterprise can give decent incomes with attention to efficiency with adequate tools and equipment and careful shaping of the operations. The tertiary sector masks much underemployment and hidden unemployment. There is no doubt that crime is fostered from history and decline in the economy leading to growth in the parallel or underground economy.

The alternative economy should be placed instead in the primary and secondary sectors. Expansion and diversification in agriculture must be buttressed by technological change and also by agro-processing especially for perishable products. Improvement in packaging and marketing will bring more opportunity and expansion. A shift to more responsibility for jobs and livelihoods within communities must be fostered with a reduction in dependence on the state for answers. That will bring a shift in economic independence in an unbalanced society and spread the weight more evenly for economic well- being. There will be opportunity for society to exercise imagination, creativity, and risk taking.

It is a country with the right potential to provide secure livelihoods for its people. A distinction has to be made between livelihoods and jobs. Promises can be made to provide jobs but that can more easily be said than done. This was a slogan produced during the last election and like party manifestoes quickly put aside as the politicians get down to business. Livelihoods can and should be put together in a self-employment drive. This is truer for a country like Guyana that faces even more pressing challenges as it tries to move beyond a traumatic, painful past. We can take 1953 as a marker for that past. The adoption of a drive for self-employment has much to recommend it rather than merely shaping ourselves for jobs that do not and will not materialize.

I have taken the liberty of repeating some information that bears repeating. While what is proposed may appear simple, it is not simplified or over-simplified. This proposal is unusual and repetition is used to clarify what is being said.

Overview

A Development Geographer studies economy in relation to people and place and the potential for growth. He/she then develops maps and models for optimal growth for that particular economy, while taking into consideration available and possible options for growth as well as limits to that growth.

In 2015, I spent seven months in Guyana conducting such a development geography study with a view towards *mapping the diversification of the Guyana economy by identifying fields of possibilities and opportunities.*

The scope of the study touched on Guyana's political and economic history, its development planning in the past — the country and its economy up to the current situation. But history is only cited in the context of a development strategy and mapping of the diversification of the economy.

When the strands of the Guyana economy are unwoven to examine its individual components, the strengths as well as many weaknesses are revealed. Weaknesses — and recommended solution options — are identified in several areas which are divided in this book under the broad heading of:

1. Mapping Guyana's diversification of its economy AND
2. Sugar is always king
3. Education: Guyana's Albatross
4. Expansion of integrated dairy farming
5. Coconut and coconut processing
6. Fruit production
7. The LGE — what next?
8. Geography, ecology land use, greening AND the
9. Conclusion

The purpose of this study and the book that has come from the research and analyses of Guyana at present is to identify the problematic areas, trace their sources and suggest feasible ways to address the negative issues. The hope is to shine the light on that elusive path to El Dorado.

Guyana's Other El Dorados:
Mapping the Diversification of the Guyana Economy

Fields of Possibilities and Fields of Opportunities

The reference to other 'El Dorados' draws a contrast between a gold rush and the pursuit of livelihoods – the latter being more pedestrian and less glamorous than the former. Many possibilities are overlooked in the 'gold fever' and these possibilities open up many opportunities that work in an economy to support society. Such opportunities open up through the creative energies of the society and they serve to anchor that society in something more sustainable.

The core concern or agenda in designing a different map for the proposed economy for Guyana must aim to increase its productivity, attain full employment and eradicate poverty. An increase in productivity must come from improved technology in the expansion and diversification of economic activity. Such technology will lead to a more labour-intensive economy. That technology may be seen as intermediate or appropriate. 'Intermediate' places it somewhere between high and low and that would make it appropriate to this agenda and the problem of capital in a poor, indebted country. Much of the simple repetitive procedures should be automated, but the intelligence and problem solving ability of the worker must be secured. It is not a case of one or the other, but both combined for the greater good or benefit. To adopt a technology-intensive approach can also be capital intensive since modern machinery and equipment are at mega-scale and at mega cost. Increased production when it comes may bring a much increased capital cost but with a much reduced work force.

Since social and economic conditions have been driven so low, it is hoped that a different approach may be taken in working out the economy. Every avenue that offers opportunity for employment and an increase in the standard of living and the quality of life must be considered even though it may seem simple and traditional. This is also appropriate under such limiting circumstances.

Not much improvement can be claimed for the Structural Adjustment (SRP) and the Economic Recovery Program (ERP) that was instituted by the IMF after 1995. The PRSP was intended to reduce poverty and become part of policy. In 1975 poverty and unemployment ran at 60%. The IMF prescriptions lasted for 20 years after 1995; Guyana continues to be indebted while unemployment and poverty remain high. These measures have not worked and another 20 years of them will produce more of the same. Allowing or making the society (labour force) the drivers of the economy can do no worse. The difficulty will be if they are so accepting or habituated to their condition that they have given up. Yet there are too many examples to show willingness and ability to find new answers and improve livelihoods. An enabling environment must be developed to make more of this possible.

The perennial economic problem in the former Caribbean plantation region has been the creation of economic conditions to put its surplus labour to work. When this seemed insoluble, emigration or export of trained nurses and teachers was suggested as the answer. In the case of Guyana emigration/export of half of its population over 50 years has intensified the problem rather than relieved it. Next, tourism has been offered as an almost universal cure to many developing countries. Tourism can be part of the answer in an economy but cannot become the whole economy. It has merit of a limited kind. A better answer may be found by examining what has already been developed to find places where further opportunities can be expanded to give a mixed and diversified economy.

Such diversification can be located in agriculture agro-processing and light manufacturing. It will be useful to keep in mind how much unemployment, under-employment and poverty must be absorbed in the expansion of these areas. More recent estimates place the poverty level at 35%, that is 35% of 750,000 while unemployment is reported as 17%. The labour force can be taken as 500,000 with 175,000 to be included in the expanded economy on satisfactory level. Since 90% of the population is located in the developed coastal region, this is where attention may be focused. This coastal region lies along the narrow strip forming only 5% of the total area of Guyana, about 4,000 square miles that includes Regions 2, 3, 4, 5 and 6. Georgetown dominates this region since it is the capital city with the national and city administration.

Guyana: Administrative Regions

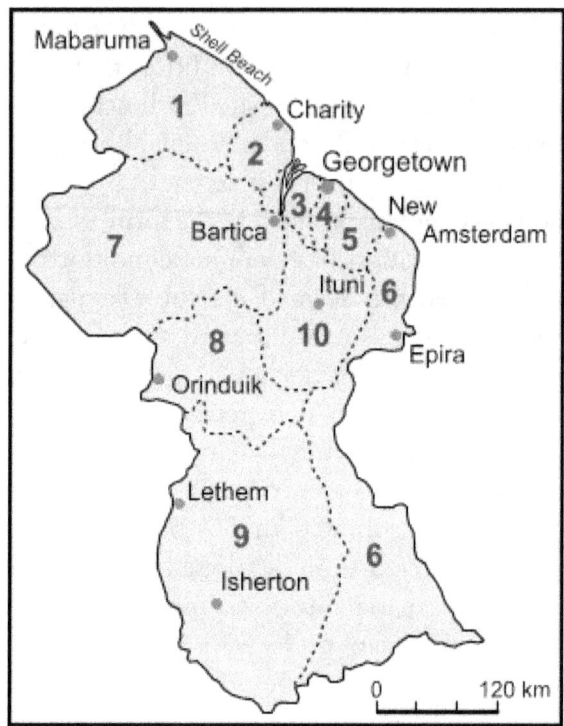

Regions 2, 3, 4, 5, 6 form the Coastal Plain

In a way, Guyana is more like the other small Caribbean islands. It is included as one of the vulnerable Small Island Developing States (SIDS) with similar problems. Yet it has much room for expansion and its natural resources are far from exhausted. Unlike the islands it has not reached its limits for further development.

Guyana has successfully emplaced itself in this northern low lying coastal strip. It is like a long narrow island stretched out over 200 miles with limited extension southward. This is its heartland and if it is seen as the first tier of development, Linden-Wismar (bauxite) and Mahdia (gold) forms a second intermediate tier of mineral and forest exploitation. Beyond lie the inaccessible mountain ranges where its rivers have their sources in untouched wilderness. The Rupununi Savanna is quite different and remote with extensive cattle ranching and a few scattered settlements. It is five times the size of the coastal region. Transport and communications are poorly developed outside the coastal region and this presents serious difficulties to the growth of the other regions separated as they are by major rivers and long distances. Much capital is needed to produce a more extensive road network reaching north-south and east-west. Because of this constraint and several more, proceeding with more modest plans may better fit the conditions.

Starbroek Market in Georgetown can give important insights to both problems and solutions. All roads lead to it with people on the move, on the hustle. The demands made on it and therefore Georgetown point to the inadequate economic base of this key city. Administrative and commercial buildings line its well laid out street system. Political and administrative buildings, head offices of banks and mortgage companies, shops and stores and service companies outnumber industrial and factory buildings. The port uses all the land east of the market and the distilling companies are on the other side of town in Diamond. There are vendors inside and outside Starbroek Market that set up shops and stalls in any space available. Vegetables, fruit of every kind as well as food and drink and clothing and cheap plastic goods, CD's, cigarettes, bottled water, fruit juice, coconuts are all on sale. The mini-bus tours and conductors are busy. The mini-buses leave loaded every few minutes along designated routes out of the city. It is difficult to move through all of the traffic unhindered and is an exercise in watchful adroitness. There are groups of the unemployed who fill up other spaces. Inside all this there are examples of small-scale innovation.

"Chicken foot" is a Guyanese creation, a crisp snack food sold everywhere by walk-about vendors. Fruit juice is sold in plastic bag containers by those who cannot afford to bottle it. Sliced fruit like pineapple is sold in small amounts again in plastic bags. Every square inch of both street and pavement is filled by vendors who pack up their wares every night.

These may appear to be of little consequence but they are examples of simple innovation. The value of such innovation must be seen for its creativity although it is not leading edge technology. There are examples of enterprise and entrepreneurship at a bigger level. Guyana does not have a public transport system but it does have an efficient, low cost mini-bus system. Private small owners have come into this space and supplied this service to serve the whole of the country. Another example of innovation in transport is the water taxi system at the Vreed en Hoop Stelling where more than 50 water taxis move commuters across the Demerara River to and from Starbroek Market. A case can be made for such initiative in the rice industry which is highly mechanized and productive occupying 60,000 hectares and in the hands of 12,000 private farmers. This started happening when the state stepped back from controlling the industry. One can speculate about the sugar industry if it too was not run by the state. Sugarcane growing could be separated into growing and processing to gain more efficiency from such innovation.

Several reasons must be advanced for a greater shift to self-employment in micro, small and medium enterprise. Neither the state nor established business nor incoming transnational companies can deliver jobs in sufficient numbers to solve the unemployment and poverty of the scale indicated. The public service was reduced by 1/3 and the 11 Government Ministries were reduced from 11 to 8 in the restructuring imposed by the IMF after 1995. This threw many out of work and deepened debt and the poverty problem.

The state undertakes to provide a range of services: safety and security, water, housing and electricity, then health and education and the welfare net for its vulnerable and needy. The bureaucracy required for the state is large making the state the biggest single employer with the largest payroll in many countries. It is enlarging the military, the police service, teachers, nurses and a host of social workers. It also sees the need for increased salaries. It has another 16,000 workers in Guysuco, a state enterprise subsidized for over 20 years to keep it afloat and continuing. The state will have difficulty making ends meet and hopes of increased state employment are poor.

Manufacturing and construction together employ 12% of the labour force. Construction may expand because spending has to go into infrastructure but established businesses are mainly traditional like rum, cigarettes, soft drinks and bottled water. While there has been some upgrading in plant and machinery, there has not been much growth into expanded markets. Although Guyana had matched Bacardi as the world's biggest producer of rum, marketing was weak. Bacardi has continued to expand but Guyana has slipped behind although vodka and 'high wine' have been added but mainly for the domestic market. This small industrial sector has to be expanded to employ more than 12% of the labour force.

The trans-nationals have directed their attention to minerals (gold, diamonds and bauxite) or to the forests. These primary activities never employ more than 4% or 5% of the labour force in most economies and use much heavy machinery to get things done. IMF conditions have given them long tax holidays and low royalties. Offshore oil will be developed for the longer term because of current market conditions. It also does not produce many jobs although they are better paid. These job prospects are not likely to produce what is needed soon enough. Neither minerals nor forests pay much into state funds; gold pays 7% and forest concessions are being renewed with no increase in rates almost automatically for another 20-year term. Increased duties on raw lumber exports have not produced more revenue. So, neither state or trans-nationals can be seen as answers to unemployment and poverty.

With such sluggish employment creation in these areas, much may come from initiatives for small activities and self-employment. Such a solution will require a great number of conditions to be met. The paramount requirement will be a radical change from what the developed world has managed. Putting together a model like this must look elsewhere than what has come out from the last century of development.

Geography, Land Use and Regional Development Focus

Since population, labour, market, transport and communications network, social services and durable economic activities are all concentrated in the empoldered coastal region, it seems logical to make changes inside this landscape. Population size is dwarfed inside the sheer size of the country. Difficulties of capital formation and investment, deterioration in education, preoccupation with crime, problems of making ends meet, a negative domestic growth attitude and so on, all forces concentration of progressive initiatives to certain areas. Areas where conditions favour success for projects of various kinds that can deliver more income, employment and social cohesion go to 'rich areas' at the expense of the poor. Outside this region, transport is only well developed from Timehri airport and Linden to Georgetown. Although the resources are there, development of the interior regions is better left for later.

Before going to the primary sector, agro-processing and light manufacturing, the question of energy production and supply must be faced. In addition to switching to green renewable energy, there is the production of ethanol and bio-diesel. Fuel and lubricants stand at 25% of all imports. Electricity is generated by diesel powered generators. Although electricity is subsidized, a kw of electricity still costs about $0.30 U.S. Kerosene and bottled propane are used for cooking. The price of gasoline is about $2.00 U.S. per litre. There is no need to say that energy is essential in all aspects of life, domestic, commercial and industrial. Cheaper energy will increase economic activity and will have a clear impact on employment and poverty second only to increase in education and training.

Map for Guyana Development

What follows here is more like a shopping list with brief notes on what could be placed on the map of the country to create momentum for further development.

Energy

1. Energy-hydrokinetic hydro systems is the leading-edge technology that simplifies run of river hydro-electricity – removes need for infrastructure since it uses direct stream flow with low head. So, green sustainable electricity is possible without elaborate generating systems. It reduces cost and comes ready to be dropped in place. Several configurations are possible. Companies in the UK, EU, Canada and India are engaged in R and D for more advances. Measurements of stream flow will determine where the systems may be placed. The Gorlov turbine is placed on the stream bed and since it reverses, it is suited to daily switching of the tide.
2. Ethanol from sugarcane juice will reduce fuel imports as will bio-diesel from coconut oil and rendered animal fats from abattoirs. These can be produced by small operations since the technology is simple and can be kept cheap.

The Economy

Agriculture

1. Dairying and small ruminant production have both a domestic market and a very large one in CARICOM ($3.5 billion U.S food imports). T.T alone imports $1 billion TT of milk products and large quantities of sheep and goat meat each year. Guyana has antelope grass that provides 16% to 18% protein. Molasses can be used to produce silage in covered pits. This can replace imported feed.

2. Feed for poultry and pigs can be produced locally, blending coconut meal and waste fish with the lowest grade broken rice—ground and pelletized. Coconut water from dry nuts to supplement feed—protein and mineral rich.
3. Increase in the consumption of local starches e.g. rice flour blends, ground provisions and the intro of lowland Irish potatoes (Jamaica is doing this) to diversify diets and reduce imports of flour.

Agro-Processing
1. Coconut oil processing, products from its fibre, activated charcoal. Coconut water—filtered and pasteurized for export
2. Leather processing, meat processing and packaging/canning
3. Candy making—boiled candy and fruit processing using invert sugar instead of sucrose
4. Citric acid—a food preservative—from molasses
5. Chips/snacks baked from plantain and banana and mango and so on
6. Fruit juices—cherry, mango, pineapple

Light Manufacturing
To supply basic needs in domestic market first and then the export market.
1. Furniture—using quality Guyana wood—Government is a big buyer. Perhaps furniture for assembly using the IKEA model with quality hardwood. Items of wood for household use e.g. kitchen and bathroom fixtures
2. Pre-fabricated homes for domestic market and for export—year round production
3. Clothing—personal and industrial to replace imported items

4. Water processing—small plants in selected locations across Guyana—charcoal filtration—made in Guyana
5. Products from leather—from imports first and then local leather—bags, belts, shoes, boots, jackets, welding gear, work gloves
6. Soap from oils and fats. Shampoo from coconut oil with aloes, haldee (turmeric), etc. Cosmetics?
7. Waste wood pelletizing from sawmills. Rice husks from parboiled mills. Pellets for barbecue, etc.

Training

Technical Skills/Regional Centres – Agro-processing/Light Manufacturing – Decentralizing

Located in the six or seven towns in the coastal regions and Linden. To include

1. Skeldon-Corriverton as both a regional centre and a bridgehead to Surinam,
2. Rose Hall-Port Mourant,
3. New Amsterdam,
4. Georgetown and
5. one in the centre of West Coast Demerara. Lethem and Bartica to be treated as special cases.

Regional centres must each have an economic base beyond services, that is, to add agriculture, agro-processing and light manufacturing in addition to their functions as service centres (administration, communications, marketing, training). Machine shops to fabricate tools and equipment; training to feed skills to promote primary and secondary activity.

The Guyana diaspora – a potent basket of capital, entrepreneurship and investment, marketers of exports, technical and other skills. Incentives for its participation/inputs?

The information given above is concise for the sake of brevity. A summary of these activities is caught in the 'map' that suggests linkages that can feed and integrate the activities more fully developed in other sections.

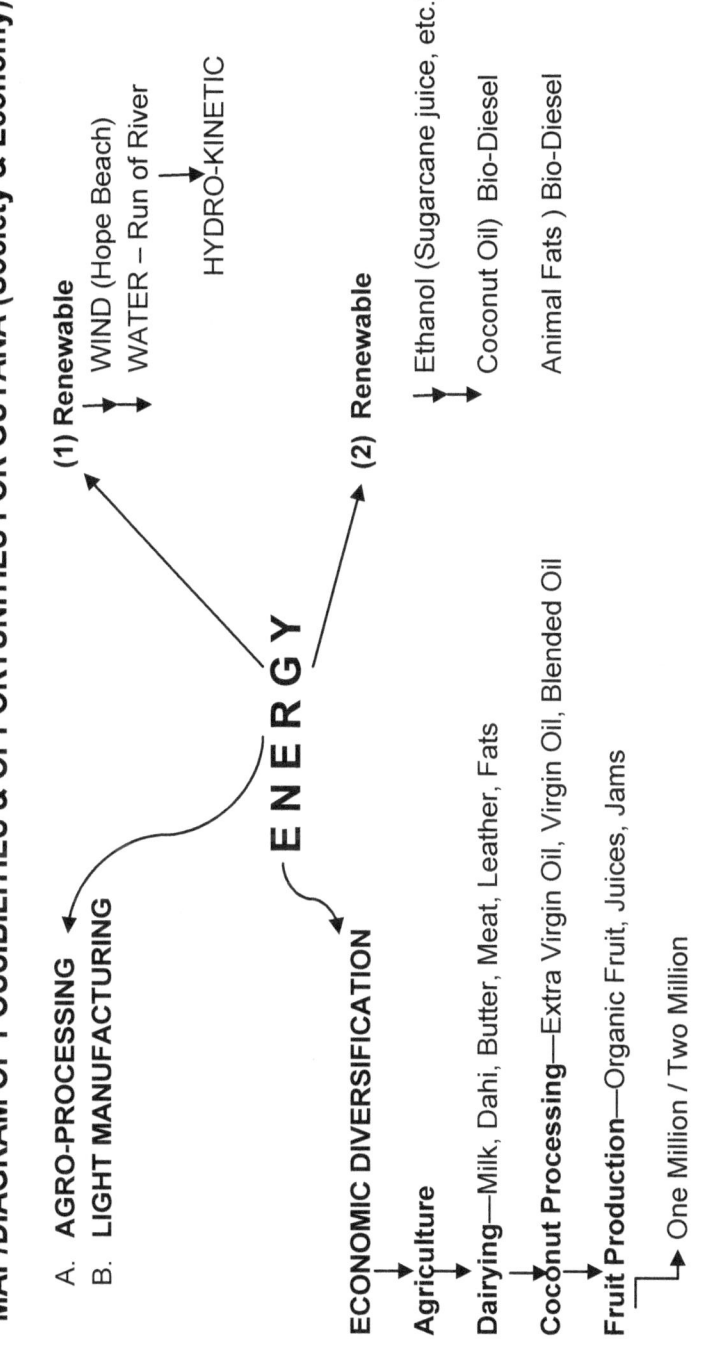

Sugar Can Always be King

Sugarcane and sugar production has become an economic problem that has had no solution either in Guyana or the Caribbean islands. There was fair warning that sugar was on the decline and in difficulty even before the end of the EU preference to the ACP countries in 2007. It is something of a challenge to say that shifting sugar from a drag on Guyana to something dynamic will be a step to ending neo-colonialism and a declaration of economic, social and even psychological independence.

Although sugarcane is declining everywhere, its value can continue to be important when its role is re-assessed in terms of its remarkable potential in a scientific and technical sense. Its sheer bio-mass productivity per year exceeds almost anything else that we grow or that grows naturally. It produces more than 70 tons per hectare. Bamboo which is another C4 plant doubles its mass in four years. They both exceed the rate at which standing forest grows and for sugarcane that is seven times more than forest trees as in the Iwokrama Reserve in the centre of Guyana. This means a great deal in terms of carbon capture and climate change. Rice and other members of the grass family may also outdo forest in this way. These may also have an underestimated contribution to make to CLIMATE CHANGE.

Its advantages in technological/industrial terms still place it high on a scale for its continued production. On a reduced or lower role, it can still supply the domestic demand as a sweetener both at home and as a raw material in making products like pastries and jams. Molasses, its by-product, is converted to rum and is an important export which has not been marketed with the success and value of Bacardi and other rums. It can also be converted into citric acid and used as an important preservative in food processing, increasing its value fivefold. Molasses already forms part of animal feed and can continue to improve the production of meat and milk. These ways of generating more cash can contribute to keeping it as a crop of choice.

There are other uses and products that can come from sugarcane juice and fibre (bagasse) than we are now making. Guyana foregoes the use of alcohol (which is really ethanol or ethyl alcohol) to reduce its import of gasoline. This can be remedied quickly since the production of rum has been mastered as long as we have been in sugarcane. This is even more surprising since Brazil is just over the border, a neighbour that has been making and using ethanol for at least 30 years.

While the two rum distilleries continue to stick only to rum with a recent sell-off of shares at what looks like a bargain price, it is puzzling when the price of a litre of gasoline has been close to the price of rum. The price of oil has fallen recently by about half but Brazil has had to make price and production adjustments for ethanol before. Between 10% to 15% of a gallon of gasoline can be ethanol – a significant savings on the gasoline imported and therefore a reduction in foreign exchange need. Up to 85% ethanol is being considered for use in cars and that will make it more of a candidate for greening the country and further reduction in imports and the foreign exchange needed. We have been making illegal 'bush rum' so why not legal ethanol for cars? A 500-600-gallon plastic tank filled with cane juice is converted with yeast into alcohol in 5-7 days. It is a bit more difficult to distil the alcohol/ethanol.

Opportunities for entrepreneurship and job creation will be opened up. Yes, it is just like making 'bush rum' but with licensing and inspection to make it legal, it should be made to work. Of course, there are the traditional distillers, but the idea is to open the way for a lot of smaller actors. The addition of kerosene makes the alcohol undrinkable so it goes only to the market intended.

Brazil and the U.S are both following up the technology of crop wastes or residues to make 80% ethanol from wastes like bagasse. These are sources of lignin-cellulose which must be masticated and made ready for conversion. Brazil's new plant for this brings a substantial investment requirement but targeted ethanol production valued in billions of U.S. dollars has made the risk feasible. Tied to this which is an entirely new avenue is the conversion of masticated bagasse by micro-organisms into a slurry or pulp to make bio-degradable paper and extruded disposable food containers to replace the styrofoam which now litters the landscape. This kind of pulp does not use chemicals which add to water pollution problems and to environmental degradation.

Guysuco, the new sugar company and a state-owned enterprise, seems to be committed to an inflexible management psychology and a determination to keep sugarcane and sugar at the top of the agriculture sector. It has been saddled with cost over-runs and teething problems at the high cost replacement of the sugar mill at Skeldon at the eastern end of Berbice. The cost of production of sugar is too high to make it competitive on the world market. There is a running war with labour that management cannot end. The state-management failure to solve the difficulties led to the recent dismissal of top management under a cloud of corruption. It is a situation where there are too many holes in the dam and too few fingers to save the day. Some are inclined to say that this is the old Booker's Guyana (colonial corporation owned and managed) or B.G. (British Guyana) not an independent Guyana in line with modernity.

Even more far-reaching and of greater consequence to animal production (livestock, small ruminants, poultry and fish farming) is the production of protein from molasses and yeast. This was first done in Jamaica during the Second World War. The protein was used to improve the nutrition value of food. It was continued in Cuba after this. Twenty-four of the 26 amino acids for full spectrum protein are produced in this process. Lysine and methionine can be added and malt and the B vitamins can also be produced. Malt production leads to other products like malt beverages. This technology of course is part of sugar bio-technology and our Guyanese chemists and bio-chemists should find this a welcome challenge. We should not have to import such expertise in a national drive to self-reliance and technical competence. Protein can be had from combining methane and ammonia as the Danes and Norwegians have shown. Nitrogen is a rather inert gas and it is more difficult to get it to react to form new compounds so this approach is much more challenging. Training in bio-chemistry and cell biology is highly desirable to allow expansion of these activities.

Such are the possibilities for meat, milk products and fish farming without the imports of corn and soya for their protein. These are combined or blended and pelletized to make the feed we need. The rice mills are now producing broken rice and rice bran; what we need is the protein to add to these. All the feed for raising chickens is now imported for example. This is the road to self-reliance and increased competence and self-sufficiency. This is part of what re-structuring and diversification must mean and become.

Sugarcane juice is also a hydrocarbon and can be polymerized in the same way as oil, another hydrocarbon. Polymerization took off after more complex oil refining developed about 1942 with thermal and catalytic cracking. Polymers are formed by extending hydrocarbon molecules into longer chains to give us synthetic products like rubber, paints and plastics. Like other technologies pollution and poisons come in this territory. While sugarcane juice and molasses offer an entry into this kind of manufacture, one must be wary of polluting the environment by introducing toxic materials into our water, air and food and the negative penalties of disregarding nature and risking our own health and lives. Negative spending on hospitals, doctors and even public health begs the question of reduced costs.

There is all of this for consideration in a development program in Guyana: biomass and climate change; ethanol for cars, etc; products from bagasse; protein production and malt and so on; nitrogen fixation by leguminous plants including shrubs, polymerization possibilities, both domestic market and export market sugar supplies with invert sugar; creating space for wider entrepreneurship; adding value to raw products through simple and more elaborate processing and manufacturing; openness and transparency for community engagement in the pursuit of livelihoods and so on.

It would be useful to make our way with as much detailed information we can find and choose. Consultation and feedback from all parties is essential to reduce cynicism and create an environment conducive to risk taking and an innovative vision. One suggestion will be to have Guysuco concentrate on processing and refining with ongoing research. It will free its hands to diversify its products as outlined above. Producing the cane will be handed over to cane farmers. Collaboration with them will strengthen the process. For example, it may then free its hands to consider making invert sugar from organic cane. A reduction in sucrose in the sugar with fructose and glucose will meet the needs of an increasingly informed consumer, who is conscious of healthy lifestyles. So, liquid invert sugar sold in bottles will have commercial applications as well in products with reduced sugar content. This is the way international markets are changing and both Guyana and the rest of the world can benefit from imaginative changes like these.

Education – Guyana's Albatross

Attempts to re-think education, for a country that shows some chance of righting itself since 1966, should receive serious and thoughtful attention. Such attention should go beyond reform and be directed to producing a generation that can find answers to its deep social, economic and political problems. The rate of change has accelerated beyond belief and beyond comprehension leaving us unable to keep up, have faith in some kind of future or anticipate and predict that future.

The last 50 years have seen the erosion in Guyana's education system with many political mis-steps that accelerated after its independence in 1966 with Burnham in power. There was progressive deterioration in education based on this English colonial pattern. This pattern had been followed all over the former British empire. The society went into greater and greater instability as the economy stumbled and racism deepened with open conflict and violence. The emigration that was set in motion took the teachers as well as other trained personnel of all kinds out of the country. Only some estimated dollar costs are given in the table at the end of this section but the other costs were very serious, pervasive and even disastrous.

The elementary schools gave important numeracy and literacy skills to the majority until just after independence in 1966. The schools were very successful in creating the base with which to manage. Many dropped out to go to work to meet the needs of the family. Schooling was the great social lever to move up in this stratified colonial world. Elementary was followed by secondary school available only in Georgetown and some towns at an expense not everyone could afford. Whatever criticism can be raised about it, many capable and competent people came out of the system. Many distinguished themselves in exile; some even managed this at home. Education slid downwards with everything else. Older Guyanese remember this earlier time with nostalgia.

Although this type of education was intended to produce conformity, some articulate leadership emerged to push for liberation and not always with positive intentions. This leads to a consideration of the type of education that can take things out of the morass into a place that has to be imagined and created. It must take young people into the real world and equip them to shift things towards solutions. A realistic handle on the difficulties that challenge their country must be kept without losing what strengths can be brought to the table. The young must be taken much more seriously by the school and their parents, and this must be reflected in what they 'do' and 'learn,' meaning that students learn skills that they will use in life. A more open education system requires many radical changes.

The 'gas station' model of education in which 'empty students' are filled with information and knowledge and then tested to see how full or empty they are is no longer appropriate. The first information explosion was recognized forty or fifty years ago with the explosion in book production. The second one came with the computer and the internet in an electronic world. While memory, correct spelling and other traditional skills are important, it is more important to learn how to access this information and interpret it and apply it.

What maps and compasses are needed to navigate through this ocean of information and knowledge? The portfolio has been added to exams at the CXC. Other changes must see the disappearance of 'lock-step' by age group with students learning at their own rate, with attention to what makes them excel rather than where they are weak. Co-operation and collaboration on problem solving, mutualism and symbiosis will characterize how they learn. Collecting current information on social and environmental problems will be guided by the scientific method and critical thinking. An exercise for students. These changes will make the learning much more student-centered, less teacher directed and more relevant.

Balancing the cognitive (knowledge) and the psychomotor (physical) with the affective domain (feeling) in the curriculum will teach head, hands and heart. The affective domain is usually under-valued and ignored. This holistic model can replace the gas station model. It could be profitably delivered through more practical assignments related to the real world, their world for which they need to learn how to find the best answers. Teachers and parents will facilitate this process by working together with the young.

This education must make society capable, imaginative, resourceful, resilient and creative, all characteristics necessary to re-build this country. Human resource development or simply education will add to a depleted cultural toolbox. That will produce the capability for development of its physical resources. More emphasis must be given to technology and science along with the liberal arts. Taking just one or two examples for mastering, there are all the great possibilities for a more scientific and technological utilization of sugarcane as outlined above. Then there are the complex challenges of becoming more self-sufficient in energy production and supply that emphasizes green, renewable sources like wind, running water, solar energy both passive and solar cell based. Wi-fi must be cheaply or freely available to allow access and understanding of these technologies and the other technologies that are needed to create the diversified map of economic activity to create work and wealth. Partly because of the urgency and partly because of a limited capacity that can be enlarged in time, simpler technologies like all those developed here in agriculture, agro-processing and light manufacture are to be chosen for practical reasons like reduced capital and simpler machines and tools. All the valuable research and expertise from technical institutions should be pooled and a list of possible activities prioritized. These institutions can do much to promote technology and vocational training with the technical skills necessary. Valuable headway has been made in some areas and offer obvious choices to choose as the first projects.

A great divide has been made between science and the liberal arts, sometimes at a very early stage. People in science knew nothing about the liberal arts and vice versa. Also, there was a feeling that training of hands fitted one out for manual labour. Such simplistic divisions deny what goes on in real life where the skilled hands of the surgeon throw a different light on things. Effective people use multiple skills to complete tasks after which other skills are used to file reports.

Since street values can over-ride the formal education that the school can supply and invisibly undermine the more positive culture of the society, it is obvious that racism and all ethnic divisions must be overcome and make way for an equitable, fair and just society. Finding the place to lay blame on others deflects or reduces the attention that must be directed to solving the real problems of the moment. It is like a teacher that quickly blames the student for failure instead of asking himself how he could improve on his teaching. At the same time, reparations may or may not be made for past abuse. History records this truth to which there must be reconciliation. The task of re-building demands learning and growing and bringing all the skills acquired to develop new strengths.

A greater percentage of the GDP is now being spent on education.

There are other services like health competing for these dollars. Great effort and money has gone to produce skilled people but there has been a substantial brain drain through which large numbers of qualified people have emigrated to the benefit of other countries. This does not add up. The table below shows the cost to Guyana for only a ten-year period. Emigration now continues at 6,000 per year. Self-employment with applied technology in small sophisticated agro-processing and light manufacturing may prove sufficiently attractive to slow down or even reverse this flow. It is desirable to build up both the numbers of the domestic population and of trained and qualified people that everyone wants. There will be many challenges for the educated and qualified to meet.

Replacement $ Costs for Emigrants – 1986 - 1996

Country	No. of Managerial, professional, technical & skilled workers	Cost in U.S. $
Guyana	14,421	95 million
Jamaica	38,582	631 million
Trinidad	8,975	178 million

Source: K.M. Bennet 1991 - www.imf.org/external/pubs

Expansion in Guyana Dairy Activity

Application of simple small scale technology and modest investment can bring desirable benefits to dairying in Guyana. The introduction of milkers, cream separators, pasteurizers and butter churns will allow the dairy farmer to manage his milk production with less effort and more technical expertise and profit. Milk and milk products will be supplied from the farm gate and/or through a co-operative to the market; marketing must be given serious improvement. A judicious measure of grant, subsidy and assistance like duty free import of equipment will get the program off the ground. That will still leave the bigger question of monopoly supply of heavily subsidized milk imports under WTO rules and the depression of the domestic milk price.

The Ministry of Agriculture believes it can solve this dairy situation with a single milk processing facility probably on the outskirts of the Georgetown region or at Mon Repos at its livestock facility. This is not good thinking for a coastal plain stretching east-west over 200 miles where the dairy farmers are dispersed. Decentralization would give a simpler workable answer. The dairy farmers would become independent small producers processing and marketing milk and milk products more effectively. This is what is proposed here.

There are many strengths already in place that can be taken to another level to permit the gains possible; such gains can bring millions of U.S dollars with additional strategies to the ones identified in this proposal.

1. There is a long history of sound expertise among farmers and agriculture support staff.
2. There are cattle of good quality. While there was an estimated total of 350,000 head mainly beef cattle, there is an adequate number of dairy cows mainly in the coastal region that stretches across over 200 miles. These are in the hands of small farmers supplying milk to local village markets within walking distance from the farm. The dairy cows seem to be mainly black and white Jersey breed able to give 2 gallons at each milking – 4 gallons per day with improved feeding and two milkings. They are strong and healthy with good udders and conformation. Some Indian cows of Brahma breed may also be good milkers though milk yield

from these may be lower initially.
3. Antelope grass and para grass together provide fodder high in protein. Feed of this kind which is widespread will produce the milk needed. This quality fodder can be supplemented with molasses and bran as required to boost milk yields. These grasses are easy to plant and love wet conditions along drains, trenches and stream banks. These grasses have spread into trenches and are seen as pests rather than the resource that they are. New blends of broken rice and bran are being offered on the market but unnecessary inputs may add to cost and reduce profits. There are options for dry season feeding from silaging, even simple pit silaging. Sweet sorghum can be introduced with advantage. It contains syrup in its stem and is crowned with seed. Sorghum can grow under dry conditions and on poorer soil. Intensive mixed integrated farming is the model to be adopted. Farms must be of adequate acreage to allow the cultivation of fodder crops of different kinds including peas and beans that contain protein and enrich the soil by fixing nitrogen. After harvesting the tops can be used to feed animals. American scale and American type operations must not be adopted without careful thought. American dairy cows are over-developed, imbalanced; while they produce some 10-12 gallons a day, they have become milk machines themselves. Over dependence on machines and fuel is not the route to follow in the face of climate change or agro-ecology. The use of chemical additives is not recommended. Such additives must be re-considered with caution since organic food is to be welcomed to the table.
4. The farm at St Stanislaus is an excellent model to be copied with modifications. It is a fine prototype but its advanced, innovative practices have not travelled beyond its gates and become adopted more widely in the farm community. Its approach is sound but farmers should be asked in what way they would prefer to adopt it; just as it is or in a form that makes sense to them. The Mon Repos livestock unit can also provide practical means and methods to bring to the St Stanislaus farm model.
5. A dairy- rice culture was common in Guyana but dairy has lost out to rice and to sugarcane too. Rice and sugarcane are monoculture farming. They each have rationalized themselves into systems

that require chemical inputs and large holdings with high cost machinery. To pump water onto a 200-acre rice farm can cost $20,000 U.S per year and it is difficult to shift rice production in any new direction. So, what acreage can a dairy farm command if it is to become viable firstly and then more importantly sustainable? The future seems to be towards organic farming based in agro-ecology rather than the big science farming of the corporate type pushed by corporate culture that thinks big, does big and fails big. Agro-ecology is based in the tried and true science of folk practice and culture which is proving its enormous unsung wisdom. Let us imagine small dairy farms of 20-25 acres spread through the villages east-west across Guyana with enough lactating cows from a herd of sufficient size to produce enough milk to give a comfortable income and living standard. A design of its layout, its equipment, its buildings, its activities as a satisfying homestead is something that must emerge from its farmers. Without their active collaboration in every aspect, they will not make this their own enterprise. Technical experts should make this part of their practice and build receptivity and a conviction of partnering with the farmer since nothing can happen without him on the ground.

6. The bottom line for domestic farm success is "what pays, stays," but that should NOT ignore the interplay of international and domestic support systems erected to give 'free trade' and an unrealized level playing field. Globalization and WTO rules are not reciprocal. [Subsidies of 30% and 40% are not removed as developing countries are fixed at 10% of agriculture GDP.] They mask the continued penetration, command and control of markets in developing countries, one-way rules that channel trade flows in a direction favourable to those who already keep all the aces in their tight hands. A serious issue is the export of powdered milk from Ireland; each ton hides a subsidy of 700 Irish pounds in its shipments. On the receiving end, Nestle's and other companies package, re-assemble powdered milk to distribute in the importing market. Domestic milk producers struggle to compete and their market slips from 10% to 5% before a zero situation is reached and milk herds slowly and carefully nurtured disappear. This calls for carefully chosen subsidies, adroit import duties, and the support for an infant industry—an option under WTO rules.

7. Should Guyana's agriculture be dominated by sugar and rice exclusively and what could diversification with durability really mean? Simple viability or a more complex sustainability—a sustainable agriculture? Bio-diversity reflects nature's amazing complexity and Guyana is equatorial not tropical, sub-tropical, temperate or arctic. It is incredibly gifted in its bio-geography—water, soils, flora and fauna —not to be underestimated and frittered away. This diversity should be paralleled in a diversified agriculture that is more, much more than sugar and rice which by themselves cannot give food security. Since the Ministry of Agriculture has a stated mission of food security with accompanying food health, milk production would supply valuable protein as part of the four main food groups. It should be pursued inside organic guidelines.
8. Tools and equipment appropriate to small dairy farming:

Milkers	$1700
Pasteurizers	$429
Cream Separator	$299
Butter Churn	$100
Total (FOB)	$2,548

U.S. dollars. Two milkers may be needed to speed up milking.

The income from sales of pasteurized milk and butter must run over $12,000 Guyana per day; 4 gallons @ 1200 = $3,600 per cow. $3,600 X 4 (better 6) = $14,400 per day. A monthly gross income of $14,400 X 30 = $432,000 per month gross. Current retail price of milk is $300 per litre = $1200 per gallon.

Income from butter and buttermilk will add to viability. Annual income can run into $6,000,000 GD or $20,000 U.S.

If 50 farmers already in dairying can be chosen to lead this initiative, the momentum should build up. The benefit of manure will improve the soil and help yields from crops grown to ensure integration. Diversification will include fruit trees in hedgerows or small allotments on the farm. Crop rotation with beans will add to the income stream.

9. Participants may be chosen for:
   a) Interest, commitment and experience with cows and milk production

b) Ownership of a suitable number of animals to have enough lactating cows in rotation to supply the daily quantity of milk to be viable
c) Own/rent/lease enough land—minimum 20 to 25 acres—to support mixed integrated farms
d) Willing and able to modify operations to suit
e) Willing and able to supply a wider market in a more efficient way
f) Expectant of doubled or tripled production and income flows including profits
g) Able to access land preparation equipment—perhaps through a co-op
h) Able to invest in the expansion necessary and meet hygienic standards
i) Able to form a co-op to gain efficiency in marketing and supplies, etc. The Co-op will give such farmers a voice.

10. Location and Distribution. Across the Guyana Coastal Plain —areas with the dairy farmers—to be trained further and led to sound profitability.

To determine a market region that will absorb the products from the farms—a village if large enough, a cluster of villages, a small town or town e.g. Port Mourant/Rose Hall, Corriverton, Kitty-Melanie-Buxton, Parika to Zeeburg, Uit Flugt-Vreed en Hoop and so on.

Coconut and Coconut Processing Guyana

Too many coconuts outside the Pomeroon district in Region 1 remain untouched, unused, unprocessed. Income (money) hangs on the trees and drops to the ground, dries and rots. We may have made much of the coconut in the past but this practice and interest has disappeared. And so an easy opportunity to diversify agriculture is overlooked.

Green Coconuts for Water

Let us distinguish green water nuts from dry mature coconuts. This coconut water has been recognized by Pepsi Cola as a far superior product to Glucozade which is offered to athletes and others as an energy drink. Glucozade as the name implies is just sugar (glucose?) to give an energy pick-up. It is like Red Bull - all hype and advertising. Coconut water on the other hand is a superior electrolyte containing fructose, protein, minerals and vitamins, and it is an organic drink. The meat or flesh removed from the nut is quality food and can be included with the water or sold separately. The problem with fresh coconut water is that it goes sour in two days even in the fridge. This can be prevented by pasteurizing to take care of the bacteria and bottling to the brim to keep out any air before capping. Additional trees can be planted and one variety produces coconuts in three years while another matures in 18 months! The common variety begins producing in five years and then keeps producing for the next 50 years. Some South Asian countries and Jamaica are already canning and exporting this product.

Dry Coconuts

The product choices are very large and varied. They include oil of three grades—extra virgin extracted at low temperatures, virgin oil and blended oil at higher temperatures. Products from the lower grades can include shampoo, soap—soft, laundry and bath soap—and bio-diesel when combined with methanol. Then there are products that can be produced from the coconut fibre/husks. The fine dust from the husk is replacing peat moss because of its superior absorbency; but traditionally by-products of coconut fibre include ropes, mattress fibre, door mats, floor mats, decorated hanging mats, and screens. The fibre can be pelletized with selected sawdust and sawmill waste for barbecues. Of course, its fibre can be used for making packaging material with the right machinery. Much coconut fibre products have entered the garden shops in Canada and the U.S. Rotted coconut husks can be combined with animal manure to supply high quality topsoil to a variety of customers.

Considerations in Vegetable Oil Production

It is worthwhile to compare coconut oil with other sources of vegetable oil. West African palm oil compares well with coconut oil for nutrients and anti-oxidants. They rank high for yield of oil. Corn and soya in contrast offer 8% to 10% compared with 70+% for coconut. Corn and soya are processed at high heat with n-hexane to produce oil which is transformed increasing their cholesterol content. This makes coconut oil a superior cooking oil which can replace the imports.

American oil producers mounted a campaign to show that their oil had less cholesterol than coconut oil. The campaign succeeded and every grocery is stocked with corn, soya and safflower oil. Coconut oil was driven out of the market but claims are now being made for the superiority of extra virgin coconut oil especially as a cure for Alzheimer's. The market for this oil has spread into the making of cosmetics, skin and hair preparations.

Plantations of the monoculture type can be avoided. Spreading the trees gives more protection from pests. There is room for polyculture and permaculture practice. Trees have been neglected and have aged beyond 100 years well past prime productive years everywhere in Guyana. A tree propagation project can be conducted not just by farmers but by youth in high schools who can take charge with appropriate training and incentives for producing all kinds of other fruit trees. Seeding, budding, grafting, air layering and even cloning and tissue culture are ways of producing new plants. Coconuts are easily reproduced by using selected dry nuts simply placed in a drain. Such activities can become an applied science practicum and make learning relevant to the Guyana environment. The goal should be tens of thousands of new trees to increase fruit production in a very favourable natural environment. We are being urged to eat more fruit as well as vegetables. Guyana has more than enough varieties including some "wild" ones that are little known.

The machinery for processing is available from the South Asian countries that have advanced into coconut production and processing. The Pomeroon exports about 150 tons of oil per year while the domestic market is not served and much opportunity for processing into many valuable products is by-passed. Abandoned stands of trees are seen all across Guyana. Rehabilitation and increase in production is very feasible. The plants are salt tolerant and does well in seasonally flooded areas. These conditions occur all across the coastal plain. This is another reason for returning to the re-planting and expansion of coconut cultivation.

Coconuts can be returned to its position as a clear money-maker.

Fruit Production

The farming of fruit is underestimated as an activity to be given serious consideration in an agricultural diversification program and as part of the economic expansion program in Guyana. Since 1980, fruit has become the second export product from Chile running at $2.5 billion U.S in value and is an important source of employment providing 270,000 jobs.

Fruit farming can be made to play an important though more modest role if its value and benefits are appreciated. Fruit has become a bigger part of the international diet since it provides more beneficial sugars as fructose and glucose and supplies essential anti-oxidants. Guyanese fruit is also produced under organic conditions not only because of the high cost of chemicals but also because of traditional culture practice. For these reasons consumption of fruit is likely to increase. Tropical fruit may have greater health advantages than temperate fruit. Sugarcane and then rice are the two crops that use pesticides and chemical fertilizers with consequent negative environmental impact. Fruit has been a secondary or tertiary player and escaped that kind of attention while still providing decent production. Its increased production should continue on an organic basis without jeopardizing the quality of water and soil. The promotion of food safety and health needs to be a high priority along with parallel food supply and security objectives. Negative spending on health delivery can be reduced with advantage while health is secured with dietary corrections.

Improvements in post-harvest handling will reduce losses from spoilage even without costly refrigeration for example by preventing bruising or by reducing exposure to direct sunlight in uncovered stalls. Cheap solar dryers made with wood frames and plastic are in use at the Guyana School of Agriculture unit for food processing. Traditional methods of processing without excessive salt and sugar should also be continued with such traditional processing methods. Such cheap well-known methods are desirable where capital is a major stumbling block in helping people to make a better living. Dependence on renewable types of energy is also to be encouraged.

The choice of fruit is impressive. They are both short term and longer term in time to fruition. Some produce fruit inside a single year while tree fruit usually requires five years to maturity. The first group includes bananas, paw paw, passion fruit and pineapple. Coconuts, mangoes, citrus, golden apples, avocado, and jack fruit (kowa) belong to the fruit tree group. Methods of propagation fall broadly into seed or cutting. Budding, grafting, air layering, cloning are forms of cutting.

A goal of 2 million new plants may be proposed but is it possible to meet such a target in perhaps five years? Placing the reproduction of the plants in schools and communities will reduce the load on agricultural institutions while at the same time spreading the business of 'development' through increased participation in the process. Too much is placed in the hands of the experts whose numbers are fewer and the community itself transfers responsibility while making itself invisible—a watching bystander. The resultant loss of autonomy and independent action seem to have made Guyanese society dysfunctional. Also there is increased need for a kind of education that replaces the 'gas station model' where teachers are pump attendants who check gauges to ascertain the success of the fill-up of knowledge. Why put off active engagement in the solution of life problems and bringing all our human resource capability to bear? There is no reason why the young at the age of fourteen or even younger cannot be made familiar with seed and cutting propagation and make serious and valuable change to their geography. They may even find better ways to go about this.

The coastal belt presents a network of sluices, cokers, trenches and drains that reflect the pervasive need for water control and management. Coconuts tolerate not only some swampiness but also brackishness. Such conditions affect this plain where salt water intrusion is a problem to rice production. While coconuts have gone to higher sand reefs they are also placed on the banks of trenches and canals and in fields that are seasonally wet. Coconuts supply so many opportunities that it should become a prime candidate in fruit expansion. Much more will be said about this separately. Dry nuts can be selected and simply set in drains where they begin to sprout before being transplanted in the locations selected. Now there are to Guyana's advantage, three types of coconuts—18 months, 36 months and five years; the first two are dwarf varieties from Malaysia. The dwarfs have been introduced to Jamaica some time ago but they can be seen everywhere in the coast plain.

Several concerns should be raised with the expansion of fruit production. Monoculture where row after row of a single plant are grown on acre after acre brings all kinds of attacks by pests that are only now being dealt with by biological answers that respect the ecology of plant systems. Yet the production of hundreds of new chemicals to spray, control and poison invaders continues, perhaps because of its simplicity, ignoring increased costs and addition of dubious qualities to the food supplied to the market. Plants grown in mixed and alternate clusters to aid convenient harvesting may be the intermediate ground. More of such plants may form the rows separating fields which will give the benefits of windbreaks and aid in water management.

Improvements have to be sought in culture methods but any review of marketing will identify the loss of all specialization producing a misuse of time and energy. The movement of goods on foot inside villages and from village to village consumes hours. The location of goods in groceries and shops can remove such problems and allow the use of effort more efficiently. That review will also benefit how things are moved around. The transport net in Guyana is broken up and incomplete. Here too waste can be reduced and co-operatives can bring many advantages. Its substantial rivers interrupt easy flow from east to west. Marketing is not helped because of spread in population distribution. Strings of small villages are difficult to serve but marketing especially in Georgetown is far from perfect.

Fruit offers quite a range in the type of processing options. Drying, salting and pickling, sugaring in preserves are simpler methods. Freezing, pasteurizing, bottling, and canning require more capital and equipment. Fresh fruit brings the biggest challenge in delivering to market in a satisfactory and attractive condition to the export market. Delivery by air is expensive and not as available. Delivery by boat and refrigerated containers is less expensive but the infrastructure requires improvements. Government inspection adds to export problems. It is all done in Georgetown by appointment, a tedious and slow business and perhaps the most serious of the problems facing export from Georgetown even inside the closer CARICOM market and then the U.S, Canada and the EU.

While increased fruit production is desirable, there are many problems big and small that hinder this. One can only speculate on their causes. It will take time for Guyana to come equal to fifty years of difficulties.

The Local Government Elections AND WHAT NEXT?

After 23 years, Guyana will again run its local government elections in mid-2016. This will bring the country on the right track back to transparency and democracy. Continued centralization of power will perpetuate more dependency in a culture which has taken many wrong turns over the years. Democracy is better served when local communities are empowered to make decisions for themselves. Sharing power with communities brings decentralization and greater effectiveness in allowing local solutions to local problems. This will bring the ten administrative regions into playing greater and individual roles in the promotion of economic and social development that best fits the geography and particular circumstances of each region. The addition of economic growth to its portfolio will counter poverty and unemployment both locally and nationally. Not only will this bring more local autonomy but it will add a great deal more of a challenge.

    The regions can be placed in two groups. The regions in the coastal area are stretched east-west for over 200 miles and have effectively developed only 5 miles in some places and 10 miles in others. Regions 2, 3, 4, 5 and 6 from the Essequibo to the Courentyne form what may be described as a long narrow island. For practical and other purposes these must be considered together as a single region, the Guyana heartland. This is the area which is most developed and that shows in the concentration of towns and settlements with 90% of the population inside 5% of a very large country. Region 1 on the other side of the Essequibo is less developed and includes the flat islands near the river mouth, the Pomeroon and the town of Bartica 50 miles upriver. Only local roads offer easier limited connection. The rest is served by boat and ferry. Although the Soesdyke Highway is paved to Linden, roads beyond are not. Mahdia is the jumping off point to the goldfields and forests of the interior and south. The Rupununi is extensive savanna thinly populated with clusters at Lethem and Dadanawa separated by the Takutu mountains. So while the transport and communications network is most developed in the coastal regions, it fades away beyond that. The problems of development are different in the two sets of regions. More is possible in the coast plain than in the interior; largeness, distance, proximity and isolation mean different things in both.

Is regional government to be orchestrated by the state or will the state empower the regional centres as agents of change to deliver green, viable and then sustainable livelihoods on a local regional basis? Local governments do not as a rule spearhead economic development embedded in the local community, generated in them, 'owned' and managed by them.

Among the many needs, the need for reasonably well paid jobs is most immediate. These jobs must come from self-employment either by individuals or by co-operatives. Self-employment brings independence in spite of many risks but nothing ventured is nothing gained. Micro-enterprise and small and even medium enterprise require capital (seed money), technological savvy and business accounting and business management. This is what a regional government can and must do—create an economic base of small activity feeding into each other.

Regional agriculture must be tailored to local environmental conditions and markets. Agro-processing will reduce rot and waste of valuable perishable produce. Light manufacturing of all kinds especially of durable consumer goods known for their quality in design and finish has a lot of room for growth. Even waste can serve as profitable raw materials. Recycling plastic bottles and rubber tires yields product opportunities. Plastic and rubber crumb reinforce the quality of hot mix for roads. Rubber crumb alone has at least 20 other uses. Such centres must be served by technical schools, machine and fabricating shops, an intelligence unit, investment funds perhaps based on social collateral that has worked so well among Grameen Bank clients, especially women.

Wherever the state has backed off, eager Guyanese have moved in and met the opening. There is no public transport system in Guyana but people have supplied that need. The state must allow the regions to construct the local economy. The state must also allow the regional bodies to collect its own taxes and/or develop financial apparatus to look after new initiatives. The state must not insist on being the main paternalistic controller of revenue in spite of all the hazards of past mismanagement and mis-behaviour in public office.

Sustainability, Geography, Ecology, Land Use

A sustainable future for Guyana raises many questions with no simple answers. Little understanding of sustainability and greening has been shown by the most senior ministers or the advisers in the President's office. Their articles in the official newspapers make promises where they show no understanding. The last budget showed even less understanding or competence. The university and other institutions are more or less silent and offer poor leadership.

Environmental sustainability implies economic sustainability, political sustainability and social sustainability. The severe damage from its politics has made its plural society fragmented. The destruction of social capital has undermined community solidarity. Elitist groups do not offer the non-partisan leadership to make responsible action on the environment possible and overcome national dysfunctionality. Co-ordinated effort by public, private and community organization has yet to emerge to manage serious natural hazards and threats.

The current preoccupation with corruption, crime, revenue inadequacy, the size of the demand for welfare, health, education, infrastructure, weak institutions and inadequate expert personnel and so on prevents broader and longer term plans to deal with the recurring floods, drainage and irrigation, drought, sea level rise and climate change in a comprehensive way. Neither an integrated coastal management plan, general land use plan nor economic and technological strategies to deal with debt, employment and poverty have been formulated.

The National Development Strategy (ca. 1997) did see the formation of an Environmental Protection Agency while it gave serious assessment of a variety of activities that were affecting water pollution, other health threats and resource exploitation. A great deal of fine rhetoric without any deep knowledge or intent from the political–bureaucracy complex appears to prevent solid action on critical societal issues.

Any action proposed does have a price tag in a country without enough cash to correct its problems. Many government offices and institutions are ineffective because of understaffing, low salaries to attract more trained officers, and a history of frustration and underlying cynicism. This may explain why so much has depended on international funding and initiation for two national parks like Iwokrama. Iwokrama sits at the junction of Guyanese and Brazilian fauna and flora systems. Recognition of this comes from cultures with more understanding and resources to take action on preservation of bio-diversity and disappearing species. At the same time, Iwokrama sits across the passageway to the Rupununi savanna and Lethem.

While international action is welcome and laudable, it is desirable that capacity and capability, environmental consciousness, effective technical systems be located in a country that is in many ways lags about 50 years behind in the 21st century. It is equally important that the society is moved to a more functional level that is, an enhanced ability to look after itself. Guyana needs more than money from generous donors. Such donors should take a more collaborative position to make the gifts of money count and contribute technical experts who will train Guyanese to take charge of projects and solve some of its own problems e.g. in the development of sustainable energy or even fish processing. Here is where a country like Norway or Iceland may take such an approach and lead the way to a different model of international aid. This may produce a Guyana that can 'act locally while it thinks globally' to make globalization mean what it has promised to do.

The geography of Guyana exceeds the capacity of such a reduced population to manage its extensive resources. This becomes very clear in its sheer physical size and its great distances. It is really a long island separated by three of its wide rivers splitting it into three or perhaps even four distinct regions. There is still only a one-way pontoon bridge connecting East Coast Demerara with West Coast Demerara across its river. The flow of traffic is relieved by the water taxis that take people into and back out of Georgetown. The new bridge across the mouth of the Berbice has replaced the slow ferry at New Amsterdam. The transport network is not complete and viable population thresholds have been met only partially in the core coastal region. This developed heartland has a rectangular shape and this is reflected in its road network.

Much of the country remains inaccessible or only partially accessible. Settlement west of the Essequibo is patchy with large unoccupied areas. While 80% of its forests still remain, the removal of vegetation in the intermediate white sandy region leads to rapid erosion and this degradation is a problem to be met. This sand problem is also present in the Rupununi savanna where slash and burn farming exposes the sand which can be removed during seasonal flooding. These ecosystems reveal this fragility. It is not enough to establish a nature reserve in the middle of the Takutu Mountains while Amerind communities fail to come of age with whatever native lore and folk science they may possess. Neither their education, technology or income levels will move them far from the subsistence levels that hunting, fishing and some farming now provides. Admiration has to be expressed for whatever ground they have made for example in eco-tourism development.

    The spill from settling containment ponds in the Omai goldfields brought home to Guyanese the danger of arsenic and mercury poisoning as fish floated to the surface and rotted. There are other problems that come from resource exploitation in the forests and mines of the interior sandy peneplain and affect both the Demerara and Essequibo Rivers bringing degradation to their basins and mouths. Bauxite mining and processing create dust, poisonous sulphur and the silt that causes sedimentation of the river beds. Dust and sulphur from calcining the bauxite causes lung problems like emphysema around Linden-MacKenzie. Tip heaps pock mark the landscape while garbage fills the holes and pond water to increase the mosquito population that bring filaria, yellow fever, and malaria and dengue and now zika. The banks of rivers exposed by mining and logging are rapidly eroded.

    The Coastal Plain is the core region of the country. Flooding, drainage, irrigation, salt infiltration, animal and human wastes, excess fertilizers, herbicides, pesticides all affect this region. Since much of the area lies below sea level at ½ or 1 metre below high tide, draining of flood water requires pumping. Canals and drains should be cleared of garbage, vegetation and silt. Rice fields should be irrigated to give two crops a year and there are periods of long droughts which threaten both sugarcane and rice. Much of it is also flat or with small gradients which make pit latrines and cess pits prone to flooding and the sewage released endangers health from waterborne diseases like typhoid. The artesian basins from which drinking water is taken may also become polluted. In addition, expensive sea defences have to be repaired. Frequent breaches are common in lower areas on the coast and in Georgetown. Since there is such concentration of economic activity, settlement and infrastructure, losses from flooding is very costly.

Energy

Energy production is the main polluter. Guyana produces no oil at the moment and Exxon will take the longer term to beginning drilling in the northwest continental shelf until the price of oil goes up. Guyana imports its fuel and lubricants usually from Trinidad and that forms 25% of its total imports. Electricity is produced with diesel powered generators. That contributes to climate change as well as diesel use by heavy machinery and transport trucks. Another contributor is the co-generation at the Guysuco sugar mill at Skeldon in eastern Berbice. Bagasse is burnt to reduce the cost of fuel and adds its greenhouse gases.

Some progress is being made for green renewable energy from the wind farm at Hope Beach. Seven windmills will produce 10% of the electricity needed at a cost of $50 million U.S. The other potential source of green sustainable electricity is hydro-power development. There are many substantial waterfalls but these are in the interior and not easily accessible. There is much interest still shown in the Amailia Falls on the Mazaruni, some distance from Bartica. This project is estimated at $1 billion U.S. Much has to be spent on access roads and infrastructure to get the turbines there and develop the transmission systems. A dam has to be constructed to give a steady flow of water. Conditions are similar at all the rich sites mainly on the Essequibo or its tributaries.

The recent improvements in turbines have been impressive. Another possibility lies in run of river hydro-electricity at smaller sites nearer the coast where the demand is highest. One choice is in the new hydro-kinetic power barge which is much cheaper and requires a constant minimum flow of one metre per second. The systems come in a range of sizes and are delivered complete to be anchored on the rivers. Such smaller generating points would be tied in to the existing grid. The cost is lower than for wind-power. The volume is large on any of the four main rivers and even from some smaller ones. Surveys of the rate of flow and other conditions are necessary. The Gorlov turbine is another attractive option since it can be anchored at the mouths of estuaries and reverses with change in tidal flow. The power is taken off a column at the top of this system.

There is a flood of ideas and information that give choices to Guyana. It is not unfair to suggest that Guyana remains passive, semi-inert and has not taken adequate action to deal with its environment. It is able to "talk the talk but not walk the walk."

Conclusion

Fifty years of independence has driven Guyana so far back that any chance of reducing debt, unemployment and poverty has become extremely difficult. Much damage has been generated internally but measures taken by the IMF and the World Bank to restructure the economy has made the situation worse. Globalization seems little more than entrenched neo-colonialism in spite of substantial debt forgiveness and a number of generous donor contributions. Active participation by the population is desirable if appreciable self-determination is to be gained and distress from economic hardship be reduced. The paths to be taken to construct economic independence must place responsibility for development in the hands of the society. That will only happen when capability is re-built in the society and when there is reduced control by the central state.

The social and psychological debilitation has been severe and long in its genesis. Racial division had been adopted as the easy means to political power. Racial hostility, distrust and disaffection run deep and undermine social cohesion and unified action on many serious problems. The rule of law has been weakened. Criminal acts have become common and the safety of every citizen is on the line every day. There are other factors that add to these difficulties. This weakening in the social fabric acts as a drag on the creation of alternative pathways to counter this social, economic and political environment and set the base for constructing a different future.

The introduction outlines the strange direction chosen by Burnham even before he rose to power after 1966. He undermined the possible sharing of power with Jagan and any racial accommodation as he rejected the shared political party formed in the early stages. Elections were rigged and the public service, the police and defence force were staffed by Afro-Guyanese. Afro-Guyanese were concentrated in Georgetown and the economy was polarized along urban-rural racial lines. Bauxite in the Linden-MacKenzie region was nationalized along with the sugar industry. Rice farming and sugar both drew most labour from the rural Indo-Guyanese. Rice also came under state control in a nationalization process that failed as economic conditions worsened and debt became permanent.

Many essential management skills had not been sufficiently developed in a country just coming out of a colonial frame and credit was withdrawn at the international level. Over the next ten years after 1985, debt conditions did not improve and the IMF and the World Bank imposed restructuring and later a poverty reduction program proved inadequate, producing a near permanent paralysis. At this time, poverty reportedly stood close to 80%. It must be repeated that the IMF approach is an accounting approach that fails to balance the books. Repeated devaluations have produced a current exchange rate of 200 Guyana dollars for a single U.S dollar. That kind of arithmetic makes it exceedingly awkward to pay the way out of debt. Debt piles on top of debt. The cost of living also makes it difficult to live under such inflated prices.

The political-bureaucratic management seeks revenue to balance the annual budget and cover the costs of its welfare net and maintain or even improve crucial services like health and services while attending to infrastructure maintenance and improvement. It continues to subsidize electricity supplies even as fuel and lubricant imports demand 25% of such costs. The state has had to reduce the number of ministries and cut the number of its employees by one third. The question then is: where is employment that pays a living wage to be created? Though the state must increase the numbers in education and health if not its own 'expert' administration, the budget cannot allow for this. It is also recognized that wages are overdue for increases.

Neither mining nor forestry ever absorbs large numbers of employees. Four percent is as high as it ever goes. Trans-national investors may invest heavily but that investment goes into efficient large extractive machinery that demands less labour. Oil production in offshore marine fields is not likely to solve employment needs and appears to be another el Dorado and a mirage.

Attention must be given to agriculture, agro-processing and light manufacturing. These sectors of the economy may just provide the employment needed if some other conditions are met. The section that offers a map for diversification shows how the employment possibilities and economic strength that rice, sugar, fish products, forestry, gold and bauxite may not be able to expand and supply. Both rice and sugar export 80% of production. Rice production is even more efficient than sugar but both of these face changing and difficult market conditions. Concerns are directed to reduction in the cost of production to gain competitiveness and that reduction may come from reducing employment.

Much faith is placed on trade as the answer to economic problems so much so that other issues on trade are ignored. A reduction on such trade dependence is not usually considered though there is much merit to doing so. That will bring attention to opportunity costs and diversification of economic activity for the domestic market and other dormant market areas. The Jagdeo Initiative to make Guyana the CARICOM food basket has fallen aside and has not materialized although that market is worth between $2.5 to $3 billion U.S. per year. Guyana does have the land and other advantages to increase food production and supply that market to its advantage. An equal faith in deliberate production based on reduced risk is desirable. This kind of 'el Dorado,' which it is not, is well worth the search and will lead to more rewards and sustainability.

Scarce funds must be directed to a more closely defined type of education that is not only technical and vocational but also directed to relevant science and technology. This is demonstrated in the real opportunities that open in the technology and science of sugarcane as well as in various other kinds of agro-processing as in dairying and coconut processing or fruit processing. The objective is to equip the society with the specifics of applied science and technology that will create a momentum for developing the projects described or similar workable projects. A consideration of various products already being made on a small-scale kitchen basis may give the opportunity to improve on them. HACCP requirements will add to their quality. These may be seen as unsung examples of modest innovation that can benefit from further innovation. Indeed, a shift from more dramatic examples of innovation driven by big capital and leading edge technology to simpler changes that belong to less sophisticated cultures may be appropriate to an exercise of this type.

The urgency of technical advances suggests that more than a transfer of cash is necessary to the Guyanese situation. Countries like Germany, Norway, Denmark and Switzerland are very able to help in a transfer of technology in areas that are unique to them. For example, Scandinavian countries are versed in the role of the co-operative in fostering economic activity. The Guyanese diaspora has acquired expertise in a range of technologies. Training institutions in regional centres can equip local communities on a collaborative conjunction that gives them more depth in this initiative. The training may be tailored to meet specific needs for local projects, themselves tailored to local geographies. Both short and longer term courses may be developed. Technical institutions already functioning will have much to add to this process.

Making Guyana independent of fuel and lubricant imports must be given priority. At the same time priority to the technology for renewable green energy would validate forests placed into protected national forests to increase carbon capture and counter climate change. The small wind farm at Hope Beach may provide 25 MW (10% of national energy needs). Run of river technology has been improved considerably. Smaller systems are now more efficient and cheaper. The hydro-kinetic version is the most promising advance. It can be delivered complete ready to be placed in the rivers and connected to the grid. The main rivers and some smaller ones have considerable volume but the gradient across the coastal plain may not provide the rate of flow desirable; a minimum of one metre per sec is required.

Cheaper more abundant energy from renewable sources will transform Guyanese industrial, domestic and commercial life. Solar energy offers another choice although storage of that energy comes with the higher cost of rechargeable batteries. Advances being made in storage look promising and mass production may reduce cost to make that practicable. Passive solar energy that does not use silicon cells has shown clear advantages from its application in the Arizona desert. Oil is used in horizontal pipes to reach temperatures over 200 degrees centigrade. Such heat is used to produce steam and run electric turbines.

What has been explored in this brief comes out of serious doubt in the global condition. The map laid out is sketchy but follows modest boundaries inside a modest practicable geography. The rich advanced world does not seem to acknowledge any limits to the production and acquisition of material goods. Service activity opens the way to limitless ascription to wealth directed and controlled by a belief "in the price of everything and the value of nothing."

Sometimes there is even reference to "the real economy" perhaps even set inside *a steady state economy*. Climate change and other manmade threats would then be interpreted differently and there would be deliberate thought given to the choice of technology which now works like a double-edged sword. A statement like "careful what you wish for; you may just get it" has haunting echoes. Can the global problem be seen in terms of the difference between *enough and more?*

Even a superficial understanding of the Guyanese situation can lead to a differentiation of basic needs and higher growth needs and be placed in a context of dignified survival. It is felt that education is a prime factor in poverty reduction and additionally produces a finer sensibility in a society led by information, knowledge and the pursuit of civilizing choices. While there should be more to 'education' than mastery of science and technology and their application in securing livelihoods, priority must be given to the applied arts where humanity still stands alongside technics to enrich the cultural toolbox.

www.ingramcontent.com/pod-product-compliance
Lightning Source LLC
Chambersburg PA
CBHW071545080526
44588CB00011B/1805